Do you know the most interesting book of all time? The one that's about you!

It's The Book That's All About YOU!

THE COMPLETE REFERENCE GUIDE TO

The Workbook For Her

An Easy-To-Use Communication Guide For Your Partner To Achieve A Successful Relationship With You!

CANDICE A. HUDDY & T. P. KENNY

The Complete Reference Guide To Me: The Workbook For Her

 For information address: Envision It Publications, LLC. P.O. Box 144, Sea Girt, New Jersey 08750 USA.

Also available: The Complete Reference Guide To Me: The Workbook For Him

The Complete Reference Guide To Me: The Workbook For Her
2010.02

Authored By: Candice A. Huddy and T. P. Kenny
Edited By: A. Ely, K. Baron, K. Goble and L. Rutledge
Book Layout and Design By: Candice A. Huddy and T. P. Kenny
Published By: Envision It Publications, LLC.

$19.95 US

www.TheCompleteReferenceGuideToMe.com

ISBN: 1449595898
ISBN: 978-1449595890

FOURTH EDITION REVISED

This book is dedicated to you!

THE COMPLETE REFERENCE GUIDE TO

Me

The Workbook For Her

An Easy-To-Use Communication Guide For Your Partner To Achieve A Successful Relationship With You!

This Guide Belongs To:

(Write Your Name In The Box Above)

Envision It!
PUBLICATIONS, LLC.

TABLE OF CONTENTS

TABLE OF CONTENTS

ACKNOWLEDGEMENTS

We'd like to thank all of our friends, family members and colleagues who provided questions, personal insights, relationship strategies and edits that have enhanced the development of this book over the past few years. We would especially like to thank the following people for their continued hands-on help, service and support:

William Butcher

Ellis Galimidi

Etty Galimidi

Ken Baron

April Ely

Scott Fcasni

The Most Effective And Useful Guide

To Achieving And Enjoying A Successful Relationship With You!

It's the book that's all about you! "The Complete Reference Guide To Me: The Workbook For Her" and "The Complete Reference Guide To Me: The Workbook For Him" are first-of-their-kind communication guides designed to help couples improve their communication with and appreciation for each other, by clearly identifying their needs as individuals.

Perfect For:

- ☑ **New Relationships**
- ☑ **First Time Living Together**
- ☑ **Rekindling Romance**
- ☑ **Retired Couples**
- ☑ **Widowed Companions**
- ☑ **Dating After Divorce**
- ☑ **Single Or Dating**
- ☑ **Busy Couples**
- ☑ **Empty Nesters**
- ☑ **Newlyweds**

First-Of-Their-Kind Communication Guides

Whether you're single, newly married, in a new relationship, dating after divorce, a busy spouse, empty nester or just looking to reconnect with your partner, "The Complete Reference Guide To Me" is the most effective communication guide to creating the foundation for a successful relationship between you and a partner at this stage of your life.

Do You Know The Most Interesting Book Of All Time?

The One That's About You!

This workbook is dedicated to you! Who you are, what you value, where you stand on issues; all of the traits that make you – YOU! No matter what stage of your life or the relationship you're currently in, "The Complete Reference Guide To Me" workbook provides a fresh perspective on how you can create a more fulfilling life for you or you and a partner. That's because the advice and answers are provided by you!

Purchase one workbook for yourself to begin a new level of self-awareness. Or purchase two workbooks, one for you and one for your partner to be used as reference guides for improving your relationship with more effective communication.

Wouldn't You Like To:

- ☑ **develop the foundation for a successful and lasting relationship?**
- ☑ **improve your communication with and appreciation for your partner?**
- ☑ **eliminate misunderstandings and assumptions before they happen?**
- ☑ **know how to handle a positive or difficult situation with your partner?**

Perfect for singles! While these workbooks have been designed to improve couples' communication as a single person, your completed workbook will serve as a guide for:

- ☑ **improving self-awareness.**
- ☑ **clarifying what you expect from yourself and others.**
- ☑ **building a strong foundation at the beginning of a new relationship.**
- ☑ **helping you identify the values/qualities you'll most appreciate in a future partner.**

WHY THIS GUIDE WORKS

Do Something Extraordinary For Your Relationship. Simplify It!

It's no secret that relationships would be so much easier to maintain if we just had a play book; a guide of "what to do" and "what not to do" based on the person with whom you're involved. Imagine a reference tool that very simply provides you with the answers you need when you:

- **don't understand the needs of your partner.**
- **simply want to do something that your partner would enjoy.**
- **can't be a mind-reader.**

The Only Guide You And Your Partner Will Ever Need

These workbooks help couples in new relationships gain a complete perspective. If you're embarking on a new relationship, finding out if you value the same things, have common goals and dreams, or if you share the same views on issues can take years to discover. These workbooks shorten the time frame because they provide you and your partner the opportunity to clearly communicate your perspectives and expectations. Knowing what you each value most and the style in which you can best communicate to be understood will empower each of you to proactively eliminate misunderstandings and assumptions right from the start. Once completed, this workbook will also provide you with an awareness to better recognize if you are in a relationship that can be fulfilling for you at this stage of your life.

Couples can easily reconnect through improved communication. Over the years, you and your partner have encountered life's issues as a couple. Yet the way in which you have each developed is on an individual basis; and situations affect and drive your and your partner's actions differently. When you both take the time to complete the answers in "The Complete Reference Guide To Me" workbooks you'll experience a breakthrough in understanding and effectively communicating with each other. That's because you'll have a fresh and current understanding of your own and your partner's perspectives. Having this information all in one place for you to easily reference enables you to produce more positive results in your relationship. What could be better?

Creating The Quick Reference Guide To YOU For Your Partner

Want to have the most positive results in your relationship? You can! Once you've each completed and exchanged your workbooks, they become simple-to-use reference guides that provide you and your partner with the most accurate insight on how to specifically relate to, communicate with and appreciate each other! Simply put, it's couples communication made easy.

The key to this guide is that the input is all yours. Take your time as you complete your workbook. As authors, we've provided you with expert level communication strategies and critical questions that will allow you to define yourself, what your values are, the way in which you want to be respected and how you want to be treated. It's the guide that is solely by you and about you. For this reason, you need to answer all of the questions honestly. This workbook gives you the opportunity to define exactly the type of life and relationship you want through self introspection and clarification of expectations. When you take your time and complete the questions in your workbook honestly, the type of relationship that you'll find most fulfilling will be revealed.

Whether you are purchasing a workbook for just yourself, you and a partner (or future partner), complete the sections in the order provided, as each section builds upon the prior. It then becomes an easy-to-read guide to having a successful relationship with you.

Important be honest and true to yourself when you answer the questions. Don't simply write the answers you think your partner (or a future partner) wants to read. Once completed, your workbook(s) will reveal your styles of communication, their associated personality traits and a fresh look at:

- **WHO** each of you are as individuals.
- **WHAT** you each value most.
- **WHERE** each of you stand on issues.
- **WHEN** you each feel most appreciated.
- **WHY** things have an impact on each of you.
- **HOW** you relate to each other and to other people.

HOW TO USE THIS WORKBOOK

Learn About, Know And Clearly Understand Your Partner

Read, read and then read it once again. Read and review your and your partner's guide frequently. In doing so, you'll more easily recognize how your and your partner's perspectives affect the way you each relate to and communicate with each other on a daily basis. Having this awareness allows you to proactively take the best approach towards respecting each other as individuals. Your guides serve as the most effective resource for you and your partner to quickly identify and understand what each of you need to feel appreciated, valued and supported. You'll enhance your relationship each time you make a genuine effort to communicate with your partner in the manner that fits your partner's style best.

Once you receive your partner's guide, begin by reading the **Guide To Effective Communication** section first. Then, as you read each of the six sections in your partner's guide, begin by reading your partner's **Quick Reference Page** first, which is located at the end of each of the six sections. We believe that by reading this page first, you'll have a better understanding as to how your partner's primary and secondary communication styles influence his/her answers in that particular section. Each time you see the **Bright Idea** symbol (shown here to the right) pay close attention. These are tips for getting "in sync" and improving communication with your partner.

Do not write, make marks or highlights in your partner's guide. If in reading, you have questions, write them on a separate sheet of paper and then make time to discuss them. The way to utilize "The Complete Reference Guide To Me" workbooks is not as a tool to point out likenesses or differences. Instead, use them as guides for developing a better understanding of your and your partner's values and how you each communicate.

Take the time to read everything and be sensitive to where your partner is coming from. Keep in mind that like you, your partner's communication style, core values and past experiences are playing a key role in the display of current behaviors. Know that you are capable of developing your awareness, behavior and communication style to create and maintain the types of relationships that suit you best. If you're ready to take a step toward self-improvement and growth, this book will show you how.

Effective Communication 101:

How Good Communication Can Build Trust

Learn from an expert. In 1990, I had the pleasure of meeting Bill Butcher, president of Butcher Consulting Group. Bill has a successful track record spanning 35 years as a CEO, top producer, executive coach, and mentor to numerous professionals. He is the founder of three successful corporations, and has taken one from inception to $20 million in sales. Bill is the creator of many copyrighted communication programs, which embody his primary principle that building TRUST® creates success in relationships. He has trained over 15,000 professionals on how to gain and maintain the TRUST® of clients, customers and colleagues. As an author, teacher and motivational speaker, Bill's seminars provide immediate positive results.

Bill taught me that being able to recognize and understand the personality traits of my own communication style, and the communication styles of those around me, would have a positive impact on every area of my life. With Bill's permission, we have summarized his professional communication strategies and applied them to improving interpersonal communication skills between you and your partner (or future partner).

Ask Yourself These Questions

- **Have I ever said something and someone misinterpreted what I meant?**
- **Can I tell by someone's demeanor the most effective way to speak to him or her?**
- **Does my body language match what my words are saying?**

First Things First. In order to improve your communication, you must first know what type of communicator YOU are and the personality traits associated with your style.

Second. You need to recognize what type of communicator your partner (or future partner) is and understand the personality traits that go along with his/her style of communication.

In this section, you'll have the opportunity to answer questions in the **Communication Style Assessment** that will help identify your primary and secondary communication styles. All of us are capable of exhibiting traits found in the four communication styles. We can also adjust our communication style to meet the needs of a situation or person. However, there will be one primary communication style that fits you best. This primary communication style is responsible for driving your values, behaviors and motivation in life. Once your primary and secondary communication styles are revealed, you and your partner will gain the valuable insight necessary to proactively adjust your words and actions to get "in sync" with almost anyone.

Let's Get Started. Complete the questions on the following pages and then follow the directions at the end of the **Communication Style Assessment** to reveal your communication style.

Communication Style Assessment

Complete the 18 questions below and on the following pages. Place a check in the box that best describes you. Select only <u>one</u> answer per question.

1. I like to:
- ☐ read. (P)
- ☐ talk. (G)
- ☐ create things or ideas. (E)
- ☐ support or help others. (N)

2. My body style is:
- ☐ thin. (P)
- ☐ medium to heavy. (E)
- ☐ thin to medium. (G)
- ☐ heavy. (N)

3. I like to:
- ☐ see things in writing. (P)
- ☐ be helpful. (N)
- ☐ talk it out. (G)
- ☐ offer ideas. (E)

4. My walking style is:
- ☐ easy going. (N)
- ☐ quick. (G)
- ☐ straight. (P)
- ☐ moderate. (E)

5. My disposition is primarily:
- ☐ dominant. (G)
- ☐ spontaneous. (E)
- ☐ disciplined. (P)
- ☐ reconciling. (N)

6. Others would describe me as:
- ☐ direct, driven, assertive and demanding. (G)
- ☐ easy-going, supportive, friendly and caring. (N)
- ☐ fun, persuasive, adventurous and creative. (E)
- ☐ conservative, quiet and professional. (P)

7. When faced with a decision I tend to put more weight on:
- ☐ the future possibilities this change will bring. (E)
- ☐ the results that can be achieved. (G)
- ☐ the information used to determine the need. (P)
- ☐ the effect it will have on the people involved. (N)

This Communication Style Assessment has been provided with permission, from Bill Butcher. See the resource section for additional information.

Communication Style Assessment

Complete the questions below. Place a check in the box that best describes you. Select only one answer per question.

8. When it comes to my personal space, home or office environment, it is:

- ☐ comfortable with fond memories around me. (N)
- ☐ functional, the phone is at my fingertips. (G)
- ☐ neat and organized with everything in place. (P)
- ☐ sometimes messy, but I clean up for a visitor. (E)

9. My personal preference for dress outside of work is:

- ☐ loose fitting, very comfortable. (N)
- ☐ practical, occasionally eye catching. (G)
- ☐ crisp and coordinated, image is important. (P)
- ☐ neat and nice but gets wrinkled. (E)

10. When discussing an issue with someone I:

- ☐ think "Get to the point already." (G)
- ☐ chit-chat first before getting to the point. (N)
- ☐ jump ahead to the conclusion. (E)
- ☐ like to have all of the background facts/data. (P)

11. When I think about my life, I most frequently think about:

- ☐ life's future possibilities. (E)
- ☐ the here and now, what needs to be done. (G)
- ☐ my past history and facts. (P)
- ☐ people I had or have relationships with. (N)

12. In a group interaction I prefer to:

- ☐ share my personal views. (E)
- ☐ issue orders. (G)
- ☐ give agreements, listening to others. (N)
- ☐ remain quiet and observe others. (P)

13. The way I make a decision is:

- ☐ fast, to move things along. (G)
- ☐ spontaneous, going with my gut feeling. (E)
- ☐ cautious with a great deal of thought. (P)
- ☐ to seek the input or opinions of others. (N)

14. As a member of a team I like to:

- ☐ direct others to get things done. (G)
- ☐ improve others so they can get it done. (E)
- ☐ be a part of a group that gets things done. (N)
- ☐ work alone so it gets done right. (P)

This Communication Style Assessment has been provided with permission, from Bill Butcher. See the resource section for additional information.

Communication Style Assessment

Complete the questions below. Place a check in the box that best describes you. Select only one answer per question.

15. My speaking can be described as:

- ☐ measured, precise and clear. (P)
- ☐ calming, friendly and opinionated. (E)
- ☐ blunt, fast paced and to the point. (G)
- ☐ caring, soft and friendly. (N)

16. To recharge my battery I:

- ☐ do nothing. (N)
- ☐ do something or get busy. (G)
- ☐ find a quiet place. (P)
- ☐ find something I want or enjoy. (E)

17. My pace at work is best described as:

- ☐ even, methodical, consistent. (P)
- ☐ energetic, meets the demand at hand. (E)
- ☐ slow, thoughtful, with breaks. (N)
- ☐ highly energetic, quick, fast at all times. (G)

18. I prefer:

- ☐ hearing the short version of things. (G)
- ☐ asking other people's opinions. (N)
- ☐ thinking about the possibilities. (E)
- ☐ seeing the details. (P)

Tally Your Answers

Count the number of times you answered "G", "P", "N" or "E" to the questions in the **Communication Style Assessment** and place the totals in the appropriate spaces below. You will use these totals to plot your score on the following page.

G ________ **P** ________ **N** ________ **E** ________

This Communication Style Assessment has been provided with permission, from Bill Butcher. See the resource section for additional information.

Identifying Your Communication Style

Look at your totals on the previous page. Place a dot in each of the vertical columns on the chart below that correspond with the appropriate letters. Notice which lettered column reflects your highest score, place the corresponding letter in the space marked **primary communication style**. Next, look at the column with the second highest score and place this letter in the space marked **secondary communication style**.

Note: We all have characteristics of each of the four communication styles. Your scores may be very close in all columns but there will always be a primary style that describes you best, at your most natural state.

COMMUNICATION STYLE CHART

	G	P	N	E
18				
15				
12				
9				
6				
3				
0				

Primary Communication Style: ______ (Your Highest Letter)

Secondary Communication Style: ______ (Your Second Highest Letter)

What Does This Mean to You?

Your communication style is the greatest determining factor of your behavior, motivation and your sense of fulfillment in life. Once you recognize the natural traits of your own primary and secondary communication styles and those of your partner, you can understand, respect and relate to each other in an entirely new way. Review the following pages frequently. Understanding the traits of your and your partner's communication styles will empower you to make a conscious effort to adjust your words, tone and actions to communicate more effectively. Read this section and the **Quick Reference Pages** in your partner's guide often. These pages will develop your ability to get "in sync" with your partner's communication style.

Important take a moment right now, to mark your primary and secondary communication styles on each **Quick Reference Page** located at the end of the six sections in this workbook. The **Quick Reference Pages** can be found on pages: **39, 63, 81, 95, 109** and **123**.

The Four Communication Styles

Style G: The "Go-Getter"

My score for this style = ___________

This style is: ☐ my primary communication style. ☐ my secondary communication style.
☐ an underlying style. ☐ a style on which I scored fairly low.

Typical Characteristics:

✓ Their basic disposition is best characterized as dominant.
✓ Their walking style/demeanor is direct, driven, assertive and demanding.
✓ Their body style is thin to medium.
✓ Their personal preference for dress is practical and occasionally eye catching.
✓ Their pace at work is best described as highly energetic, quick and fast at all times.

Approach To Decision Making And Problem Solving:

✓ When faced with a decision they put more weight on the results that can be achieved.
✓ When making a decision they are fast to move things along.
✓ To problem solve they like to talk it out.

Personal Space And Downtime Needs:

✓ When it comes to their personal space they like things to be functional, with things at their fingertips.
✓ To recharge their battery they do something or get busy.

Communication Needs:

✓ They typically like to talk.
✓ Their speaking style can be described as blunt, fast paced and to the point.
✓ They prefer hearing the short version of things.
✓ When discussing an issue with someone they think "Get to the point already."
✓ When thinking about their life they most frequently think about the "here and now," what they need to do.

Relating To Others:

✓ As a member of a team they direct others to get things done.
✓ In group interactions they prefer to issue orders.

This content has been summarized with permission, from Bill Butcher. See the resource section for additional information.

The Four Communication Styles

"Go-Getter" Style Communicators

Positive Personality Traits:

- Decided, definitive and determined to complete things.
- Goal/ results oriented, achievement driven and efficient.
- Independent, they take initiative, they are self-starters.
- Risk takers, adventurous and competitive.
- They enjoy variety and challenges.

Negative Personality Traits:

- Poor listeners, impatient and blunt.
- Impulsive, bored by routine and restless.
- They fear inactivity, relaxation and being unproductive.
- Insensitive because projects and outcomes are more important than people.

Cues That You Are "Out Of Sync" When Communicating With Them:

- They take over or dictate what they want because they don't feel you're taking action.

Note: They need to HEAR things. Their way of communicating is primarily AUDITORY.

Communication Tip: Speak in short sentences; get right to the point; mention what you expect of them; the outcome to be achieved and the deadline.

This content has been summarized with permission, from Bill Butcher. See the resource section for additional information.

The Four Communication Styles

Style P: The "Perfectionist"

My score for this style = __________

This style is:
- ☐ my primary communication style.
- ☐ my secondary communication style.
- ☐ an underlying style.
- ☐ a style on which I scored fairly low.

Typical Characteristics:

✓ Their basic disposition is best characterized as disciplined.
✓ Their walking style/demeanor is conservative, straight, quiet and professional.
✓ Their body style is thin.
✓ Their personal preference for dress is crisp and coordinated, they believe that image is everything.
✓ Their pace at work is best described as even, methodical and consistent.

Approach To Decision Making And Problem Solving:

✓ When faced with a decision they put more weight on the data and process used to determine the need.
✓ When making a decision they are cautious, putting a great deal of thought into their decisions.
✓ To problem solve they like to see things in writing.

Personal Space And Downtime Needs:

✓ When it comes to their personal space they like things to be neat, organized with everything in its place.
✓ To recharge their battery they find a quiet place.

Communication Needs:

✓ They typically like to read.
✓ Their speaking style can be described as measured, precise and clear.
✓ They prefer seeing the details.
✓ When discussing an issue with someone they want all of the background, data and facts.
✓ When thinking about their life they most frequently think about their past, history and facts.

Relating To Others:

✓ As a member of a team they are self-reliant, working alone so things get done "right."
✓ In group interactions they prefer to remain quiet and observe others.

This content has been summarized with permission, from Bill Butcher. See the resource section for additional information.

The Four Communication Styles

"Perfectionist" Style Communicators

Positive Personality Traits:

- Detail oriented, thorough, orderly and methodical.
- Good at maintaining exceptionally high standards.
- Industrious, fixated on details, analytical and controlled.
- Intuitive, accurate, slow, calm and precise.

Negative Personality Traits:

- Perfectionists, hard on themselves and can be critical of others.
- Picky, overly cautious and overly sensitive.
- They may take constructive criticism personally.
- Resistant to change, stubborn, not making decisions without "all" of the facts.

Cues That You Are "Out Of Sync" When Communicating With Them:

- They withdraw, become silent and nod a lot because they don't feel you believe them.

Note: They need to SEE things. Their way of communicating is primarily VISUAL.

Communication Tip: Be thorough when you are speaking. Refer to things, beginning with the past and working toward the present. If possible put things in writing and slow your pace when speaking. Provide logical and orderly details.

This content has been summarized with permission, from Bill Butcher. See the resource section for additional information.

The Four Communication Styles

Style E: The "Enthusiast"

My score for this style = ____________

This style is: ☐ my primary communication style. ☐ my secondary communication style.
☐ an underlying style. ☐ a style on which I scored fairly low.

Typical Characteristics:

✓ Their basic disposition is best characterized as spontaneous.
✓ Their walking style/demeanor is fun, persuasive, adventurous and creative.
✓ Their body style is medium to full.
✓ Their personal preference for dress is neat and nice but gets wrinkled.
✓ Their pace at work is best described as energetic, meeting the demand at hand.

Approach To Decision Making And Problem Solving:

✓ When faced with a decision they put more weight on the future possibilities it will bring.
✓ When making a decision they are spontaneous, going with their gut feeling or using intuition.
✓ To problem solve they like to offer ideas.

Personal Space And Downtime Needs:

✓ When it comes to their personal space they like things to be all around them but will clean up for a visitor.
✓ To recharge their battery they find something to do that they enjoy.

Communication Needs:

✓ They typically like to create things or ideas.
✓ Their speaking style can be described as calming, friendly and opinionated.
✓ They prefer thinking about the possibilities.
✓ When discussing an issue with someone they jump ahead to the conclusion.
✓ When thinking about their life they most frequently think about life's future possibilities.

Relating To Others:

✓ As a member of a team they improve or teach others so the team can get things done.
✓ In group interactions they prefer to share their personal views.

This content has been summarized with permission, from Bill Butcher. See the resource section for additional information.

The Four Communication Styles

"Enthusiast" Style Communicators

Positive Personality Traits:

- Optimistic, enthusiastic and motivating.
- Passionate, emotional and dramatic.
- Fun loving, outgoing and personable.
- Engaging and communicating effectively.

Negative Personality Traits:

- Reactive, impulsive and overly emotional.
- Disorganized, too talkative and unrealistic.
- They disregard details.

Cues That You Are "Out Of Sync" When Communicating With Them:

- They'll turn the situation around on you because they feel attacked.

Note: They need to IMAGINE things. Their way of communicating is primarily INTUITIVE.

Communication Tip: Begin your conversation with "the vision" you have for something to involve them in. Ask them about their ideas and what rewards the outcome can bring to them. Be friendly and excited about the topic you're discussing.

This content has been summarized with permission, from Bill Butcher. See the resource section for additional information.

The Four Communication Styles

Style N: The "Nurturer"

My score for this style = __________

This style is:
- ☐ my primary communication style.
- ☐ my secondary communication style.
- ☐ an underlying style.
- ☐ a style on which I scored fairly low.

Typical Characteristics:

- ✓ Their basic disposition is best characterized as reconciling.
- ✓ Their walking style/demeanor is easy-going, supportive, friendly and caring.
- ✓ Their body style is full.
- ✓ Their personal preference for dress is loose fitting and very comfortable.
- ✓ Their pace at work is best described as slow and thoughtful with breaks.

Approach To Decision Making And Problem Solving:

- ✓ When faced with a decision they put more weight on the effect it will have on the people involved.
- ✓ When making a decision they first seek the input and opinions of others.
- ✓ To problem solve they like to be helpful.

Personal Space And Downtime Needs:

- ✓ When it comes to their personal space they like things to be comfortable with fond memories around.
- ✓ To recharge their battery they do nothing.

Communication Needs:

- ✓ They typically like to support or help others.
- ✓ Their speaking style can be described as caring, soft and friendly.
- ✓ They prefer asking other people's opinions.
- ✓ When discussing an issue with someone they will chit-chat first then eventually get to the point.
- ✓ When thinking about their life they most frequently think about people and relationships they have.

Relating To Others:

- ✓ As a member of a team they like to be a part of a group that gets things done.
- ✓ In group interactions they prefer to give agreements and listen to others speak.

This content has been summarized with permission, from Bill Butcher. See the resource section for additional information.

The Four Communication Styles

"Nurturer" Style Communicators

Positive Personality Traits:

- Dependable, reliable, a real team player.
- Stable, empathetic and tremendously loyal.
- Compassionate and sensitive to others.
- Patient, easy-going and supportive.

Negative Personality Traits:

- Stubborn. They hold grudges and they recall the hurts inflicted by others.
- Indecisive. They are slow to initiate and they fear change.
- Overly accommodating to the demands of others.
- Non-reactive, they avoid confrontation and they sacrifice results for the sake of people.

Cues That You Are "Out Of Sync" When Communicating With Them:

- They give you a lot of "yeses" because they don't feel you are "with them" as a team.

Note: They need to FEEL SECURE. Their way of communicating is primarily FEELING.

Communication Tip: Begin your conversation with how both of you can achieve or do something together. Be friendly and calm in your discussion focusing on the ease of tasks.

This content has been summarized with permission, from Bill Butcher. See the resource section for additional information.

WHO I AM

When You Complete This Section <u>You</u> Will Learn:

- ✓ How You Define Yourself
- ✓ What You Expect From Yourself And Others

<u>Section Goal:</u> Clarify Your Core Values

Have you ever taken the time to define who you are? This section is intended to help you clarify your core values and see how these values ultimately drive your behavior and outlook. Once completed, this section will provide you and your partner with a snapshot of how you define yourself and what you really want out of life. This information will give your partner a whole new perspective as to how he/she can understand and support what it takes for you to achieve a sense of fulfilment.

When You Exchange Your Workbook, <u>Your Partner</u> Will Learn:

WHO I AM

My Personality Traits

For the most part I am a person who:	☐ is a planner.		☐ lives day by day.
For the most part I am a person who is:	☐ a peacekeeper.		☐ a change agent.
When making decisions I mostly use:	☐ logic.		☐ emotions.
I consider myself to be relatively:	☐ non-adventurous.		☐ adventurous.
In a work situation that has deadlines, I:	☐ don't respond well.		☐ thrive.
In a personal situation that has deadlines, I:	☐ don't respond well.		☐ thrive.
I have a tendency to take constructive criticism:	☐ for what it is.		☐ personally.
I have a tendency to take accolades:	☐ for what they are.		☐ personally.

I am someone who adapts easily to change.	☐ yes		☐ no
I consider myself to be handy.	☐ yes		☐ no
I'm consistent with how most people my age act.	☐ yes		☐ no
I work better with a team.	☐ yes		☐ no
I am typically a leader.	☐ yes		☐ no
I typically wear my heart on my sleeve.	☐ yes		☐ no
My life is an open book for all to read.	☐ yes		☐ no
I love to meet new people.	☐ yes		☐ no
I typically go out of my way to help others.	☐ yes		☐ no
I remind others how much I appreciate them.	☐ yes		☐ no
My closest friends share the same values as I do.	☐ yes		☐ no
I have the same or similar values as my mentors.	☐ yes		☐ no

I tend to stay out all night.	☐ rarely	☐ sometimes	☐ often
I tend to do my best work in the:	☐ morning.	☐ afternoon.	☐ evening.
For the most part I am a person who is:	☐ a realist.	☐ an optimist.	☐ a pessimist.

My Personality Traits

In a crisis situation, my typical reaction is to be: (Check all that apply.)

- ☐ calm.
- ☐ a leader.
- ☐ helpful.
- ☐ nervous.
- ☐ a troubleshooter.
- ☐ caring/kind.
- ☐ frantic.
- ☐ frozen.
- ☐ ______________________.

I have a natural tendency to be: (Check all that apply.)

- ☐ compulsive.
- ☐ unrealistic.
- ☐ self-conscious.
- ☐ judgmental.
- ☐ aloof/detached.
- ☐ a perfectionist.
- ☐ erratic.
- ☐ uninspired.
- ☐ driven.
- ☐ moody.
- ☐ unsettled.
- ☐ ______________________.

It's difficult for me to relate to or deal with people who are:

____

Things people do that make me respect them are:

____

Things people do that impress me are:

____

Traits about myself that I am proud of are:

____

Physical attributes about myself that I feel insecure about are:

____

Something you would never guess about me is:

____

My number one flaw is:

____

My quirkiest behavior is:

____

My Personality Traits

Check the top 10 answers that best apply or add your own answer where applicable.

I consider myself to be someone who is or can be:

- ☐ easy going.
- ☐ controlling.
- ☐ determined.
- ☐ confident.
- ☐ close minded.
- ☐ committed.
- ☐ solemn.
- ☐ quiet/shy.
- ☐ outgoing.
- ☐ peaceful.
- ☐ a drifter.
- ☐ arrogant.
- ☐ open minded.
- ☐ loyal.
- ☐ stressed.
- ☐ joyful.
- ☐ careless.
- ☐ caring/kind.
- ☐ laid back.
- ☐ happy.
- ☐ virtuous.
- ☐ honest.
- ☐ dramatic.
- ☐ serious.
- ☐ high strung.
- ☐ competitive.
- ☐ intimidating.
- ☐ indifferent.
- ☐ aloof.
- ☐ genuine.
- ☐ comedic.
- ☐ ______________________.

People at work tend to see or perceive me to be someone who is or can be:

- ☐ easy going.
- ☐ controlling.
- ☐ determined.
- ☐ confident.
- ☐ close minded.
- ☐ committed.
- ☐ solemn.
- ☐ quiet/shy.
- ☐ outgoing.
- ☐ peaceful.
- ☐ a drifter.
- ☐ arrogant.
- ☐ open minded.
- ☐ loyal.
- ☐ stressed.
- ☐ joyful.
- ☐ careless.
- ☐ caring/kind.
- ☐ laid back.
- ☐ happy.
- ☐ virtuous.
- ☐ honest.
- ☐ dramatic.
- ☐ serious.
- ☐ high strung.
- ☐ competitive.
- ☐ intimidating.
- ☐ indifferent.
- ☐ aloof.
- ☐ genuine.
- ☐ comedic.
- ☐ ______________________.

My friends and family tend to see or perceive me to be someone who is or can be:

- ☐ easy going.
- ☐ controlling.
- ☐ determined.
- ☐ confident.
- ☐ close minded.
- ☐ committed.
- ☐ solemn.
- ☐ quiet/shy.
- ☐ outgoing.
- ☐ peaceful.
- ☐ a drifter.
- ☐ arrogant.
- ☐ open minded.
- ☐ loyal.
- ☐ stressed.
- ☐ joyful.
- ☐ careless.
- ☐ caring/kind.
- ☐ laid back.
- ☐ happy.
- ☐ virtuous.
- ☐ honest.
- ☐ dramatic.
- ☐ serious.
- ☐ high strung.
- ☐ competitive.
- ☐ intimidating.
- ☐ indifferent.
- ☐ aloof.
- ☐ genuine.
- ☐ comedic.
- ☐ ______________________.

Childish things I sometimes do are:

______________________________ ______________________________

______________________________ ______________________________

My Outlook On Life

Things that make me smile are:

I think the purpose of my life is:

Things or situations that make me feel sad are:

Things or situations that make me feel guilty are:

Something that I am proud of is:

Something that I am not so proud of is:

My biggest passion is:

WHO I AM

My Priorities

The five most important things in my life are: (Put in order with 1 indicating your TOP priority.)

1. ______________________________
2. ______________________________
3. ______________________________
4. ______________________________
5. ______________________________

Those in my life who are priorities are: (Put in order with 1 indicating your TOP priority.)

____ friends ____ immediate family ____ mentors ____ co-workers
____ relatives ____ peer group ____ pets ____ ______________

I typically believe people in general are: ☐ good natured. ☐ opportunistic.

I typically see the glass as: ☐ half full. ☐ half empty.

If I could improve one thing in society it would be:

____
____
____

The way I want people to think of me or remember me is:

____
____
____

I typically look for these qualities in my friends:

______________ ______________
______________ ______________
______________ ______________

What Inspires Me

I look for these qualities in my mentors:

I look for these qualities in a partner:

Role models in my life are:

Mentors in my life are:

Things that motivate or inspire me are:

My Downtime And Personal Space

When in a conversation, the spacial distance I am most comfortable keeping between myself and

my family is:

☐ close. ☐ at arm's length. ☐ further than arm's length.

my friends is:

☐ close. ☐ at arm's length. ☐ further than arm's length.

my colleagues is:

☐ close. ☐ at arm's length. ☐ further than arm's length.

new acquaintances is:

☐ close. ☐ at arm's length. ☐ further than arm's length.

When I'm feeling sick or not well, I usually need:

____

____

____

When I'm feeling stressed or overwhelmed, I most likely need:

____

____

____

When I'm feeling sad or depressed, I generally need:

____

____

____

When I'm feeling angry, I need:

____

____

____

My Downtime And Personal Space

On the weekends I usually like to:

☐ sleep late. ☐ get up early. ☐ take each day as it comes.

I am the kind of person who needs to sleep:

☐ 4-6 hours. ☐ 6-8 hours. ☐ 8+ hours.

The amount of daily alone time I need is:

☐ 1-4 hours. ☐ 4-8 hours. ☐ more than 8 hours.

My sleep pattern tends to be:

☐ light. ☐ deep. ☐ restless. ☐ ____________________.

If I have to share my bed, I prefer to sleep:

☐ on the left side. ☐ on the right side. ☐ near a door. ☐ near a window.
☐ close together. ☐ with space. ☐ near a phone. ☐ ____________________.

An ideal temperature for me to sleep well is:

☐ moderate. ☐ hot. ☐ windows open. ☐ cool.
☐ with a fan. ☐ cold. ☐ very cold. ☐ ____________________.

Pet peeves of mine related to sleeping are:

______________________________ ______________________________
______________________________ ______________________________
______________________________ ______________________________

The way I handle it if someone is snoring is:

____
____
____

My Habits "Good And Not So Good"

Good habits I am trying to develop are:

Bad habits I am trying to break are:

Pet peeves of mine when it comes to other people's bad habits:

The importance of my own personal hygiene and that of others is:

☐ somewhat important. ☐ very important. ☐ unimportant.

I make an effort in my overall grooming to be:

☐ meticulous. ☐ casual. ☐ unimportant.

Before going to a special occasion, I do the following as it relates to my personal grooming:

Pet peeves of mine as it relates to others' personal grooming:

My Habits "Good And Not So Good"

My table manners are:

☐ informal. ☐ semi-formal. ☐ formal. ☐ unimportant to me.

My business etiquette is:

☐ informal. ☐ semi-formal. ☐ formal. ☐ unimportant to me.

My social etiquette is:

☐ informal. ☐ semi-formal. ☐ formal. ☐ unimportant to me.

I exercise or work out:

☐ rarely. ☐ sometimes. ☐ often. ☐ unimportant to me.

I am a healthy eater – my meals are well balanced:

☐ rarely. ☐ sometimes. ☐ often. ☐ unimportant to me.

I take vitamins and drink adequate amounts of water:

☐ rarely. ☐ sometimes. ☐ often. ☐ unimportant to me.

I see a physician or dentist proactively:

☐ rarely. ☐ sometimes. ☐ often. ☐ unimportant to me.

Key concerns I have relating to my physical condition are:

______________________________ ______________________________
______________________________ ______________________________
______________________________ ______________________________

Key concerns I have relating to my family health history are:

______________________________ ______________________________
______________________________ ______________________________
______________________________ ______________________________

My Values And Beliefs

What I value in life most is:

What I value in people is:

My idea of being loyal is:

People to whom I am loyal are:

I believe accountability means:

My definition of responsibility is:

To have integrity means:

My Values And Beliefs

Being respectful means:

My idea of being "in love" is:

Being in an exclusive relationship means:

My definition of honesty is:

I believe to have good character means:

To love someone means:

My three closest friends at this stage of my life are:

My Values And Beliefs

I define lying as:

I define cheating in a relationship as:

My idea of being faithful is:

My idea of being unfaithful or betraying someone's trust is:

The way I deal with people who break or betray my trust is:

I define success as:

Things I Want To Accomplish

Skills I'd like to develop:

Places I'd like to visit:

Things I'd like to acquire:

People I'd like to meet:

Experiences I'd like to have:

Things I Want To Accomplish

Things I want to do or accomplish within one year:

Things I want to do or accomplish within five years:

Things I want to do or accomplish within ten years:

Communication Tip: Learn the personality traits of your partner's primary and secondary communication styles below. You'll gain new insight as to how the traits of her communication styles have an impact on her answers in the **Who I Am** section.

Go-Getter Traits

This style is: ☐ my primary style. ☐ my secondary style.

Appearance: practical, to create dialogue
Degree of formality: low, informal
Body movement/tempo: fast
Relaxation level: low
Facial expression: anticipatory

Environment: set up for sounds and talking
Voice pitch: medium, crystal clear
Posture: leans forward, aggressive
Gait of speech: fast, to the point
Sense of urgency: high, action oriented

Perfectionist Traits

This style is: ☐ my primary style. ☐ my secondary style.

Appearance: color coordinated, well-groomed
Degree of formality: high, formal
Body movement/tempo: deliberate
Relaxation level: moderate
Facial expression: serious

Environment: neat, organized, professional
Voice pitch: high
Posture: sits up straight, disciplined
Gait of speech: deliberate
Sense of urgency: moderate, orderly

Enthusiast Traits

This style is: ☐ my primary style. ☐ my secondary style.

Appearance: comfortable, non-conventional
Degree of formality: moderate
Body movement/tempo: energetic
Relaxation level: energetic
Facial expression: alert, quick to smile

Environment: functional, convenient
Voice pitch: low, calm
Posture: comfortable, alert
Gait of speech: dynamic, vigorous
Sense of urgency: spontaneous

Nurturer Traits

This style is: ☐ my primary style. ☐ my secondary style.

Appearance: comfort, soft fabrics
Degree of formality: low, casual
Body movement/tempo: slow, easy going
Relaxation level: high, comfortable
Facial expression: calm, soft smile

Environment: comfort, relaxed, memories
Voice pitch: low, caring, sensitive
Posture: comfortable, relaxed
Gait of speech: slow, calm
Sense of urgency: low, relaxed

WHAT I VALUE

When You Complete This Section <u>You</u> Will Learn:

- ✓ **What You Most Enjoy Doing Is Based On What You Value**
- ✓ **What New Interests You're Willing To Consider**

<u>Section Goal:</u> Schedule Some Happiness

Have you ever really thought about what brings you joy? This section is intended to reveal whether or not you are incorporating into your daily routine the interests and activities that bring you happiness. As an individual, you owe it to yourself to plan regular activities that will enhance your sense of self-fulfilment. The answers to the following questions will make it easy for you and your partner to genuinely plan an activity, special event or simply a night out that you'll both value and enjoy.

When You Exchange Your Workbook, <u>Your Partner</u> Will Learn:

Our Initial Compatibility

When it comes to my partner, I am most attracted to these qualities:

When it comes to my partner, I am most attracted to these personality traits/mannerisms:

When it comes to my partner, I am most attracted to these physical traits:

I am naturally drawn to people with these career goals:

I am naturally drawn to people with an outlook on life that includes:

Our Initial Compatibility

The level of importance to me that my partner and I share the same career goals and work ethic is:
☐ unimportant. ☐ somewhat important. ☐ extremely important.

The level of importance to me that my partner and I share a similar outlook on life is:
☐ unimportant. ☐ somewhat important. ☐ extremely important.

The level of importance to me that my partner and I share similar political views is:
☐ unimportant. ☐ somewhat important. ☐ extremely important.

The level of importance to me that my partner and I share similar religious beliefs and practices are:
☐ unimportant. ☐ somewhat important. ☐ extremely important.

The level of importance to me that my partner and I share the same level of education is:
☐ unimportant. ☐ somewhat important. ☐ extremely important.

The level of importance to me that my partner and I share similar views on managing our finances is:
☐ unimportant. ☐ somewhat important. ☐ extremely important.

The level of importance to me that my partner and I share similar views of raising a family is:
☐ unimportant. ☐ somewhat important. ☐ extremely important.

The level of importance to me that my partner and I share similar definitions of how we have fun is:
☐ unimportant. ☐ somewhat important. ☐ extremely important.

The level of importance to me that my partner and I share similar views on what we bring to and expect from a relationship is:
☐ unimportant. ☐ somewhat important. ☐ extremely important.

The level of importance to me that my partner and I share similar opinions on the amount of time we enjoy spending together or apart is:
☐ unimportant. ☐ somewhat important. ☐ extremely important.

WHAT I VALUE

Our Initial Compatibility

Check <u>one</u> answer per line. (Use 1 to indicate what is <u>LEAST</u> important to you and 4 to indicate what is <u>MOST</u> important to you.)

It is important to me that intellectually my partner and I:

have a lot to talk about.	___ 1	___ 2	___ 3	___ 4
are on the same wave length.	___ 1	___ 2	___ 3	___ 4
respect each other's way of thinking.	___ 1	___ 2	___ 3	___ 4
are intellectually stimulated by each other.	___ 1	___ 2	___ 3	___ 4

It is important to me that emotionally my partner:

makes me feel listened to.	___ 1	___ 2	___ 3	___ 4
feels my needs are important.	___ 1	___ 2	___ 3	___ 4
accepts the way I do things.	___ 1	___ 2	___ 3	___ 4
makes me feel cared about.	___ 1	___ 2	___ 3	___ 4
makes me feel comfortable.	___ 1	___ 2	___ 3	___ 4
is dependable.	___ 1	___ 2	___ 3	___ 4
enjoys his/her time with me.	___ 1	___ 2	___ 3	___ 4
respects me as a person first, then as his/her partner.	___ 1	___ 2	___ 3	___ 4
is proud of me.	___ 1	___ 2	___ 3	___ 4
cherishes or admires me.	___ 1	___ 2	___ 3	___ 4
believes that I enhance his/her life in some way.	___ 1	___ 2	___ 3	___ 4

Physical chemistry is important, therefore it is important that my partner:

keeps up his/her appearance.	___ 1	___ 2	___ 3	___ 4
is excited about spending time with me.	___ 1	___ 2	___ 3	___ 4
is physically attracted to me.	___ 1	___ 2	___ 3	___ 4
fantasizes about me.	___ 1	___ 2	___ 3	___ 4
and I have an active romantic life.	___ 1	___ 2	___ 3	___ 4
understands my romantic needs.	___ 1	___ 2	___ 3	___ 4

It is important to me that spiritually my partner and I:

have similar spiritual beliefs and/or philosophies.	___ 1	___ 2	___ 3	___ 4

WHAT I VALUE

My General Likes And Dislikes

A nickname I like:

and one I hate:

Events I enjoy attending:

and ones I don't:

Exciting things I've ever done:

and the scariest:

Types of exercise I enjoy:

and ones I don't:

Family traditions I love:

and ones I don't:

Topics I enjoy discussing:

and ones I don't:

Occasions I enjoy getting dressed up for:

and ones I don't:

WHAT I VALUE

My General Likes And Dislikes

My work attire could best be described as:

- ☐ Trendy.
- ☐ Classic.
- ☐ International.
- ☐ Preppy.
- ☐ Western.
- ☐ Club.
- ☐ Corporate Casual.
- ☐ T-shirt and Blue Jeans.
- ☐ Bohemian/Artistic.
- ☐ Skate/Surf.
- ☐ Flashy.
- ☐ Assigned Uniform.

My non-work attire could best be described as:

- ☐ Trendy.
- ☐ Classic.
- ☐ International.
- ☐ Preppy.
- ☐ Western.
- ☐ Club.
- ☐ Corporate Casual.
- ☐ T-shirt and Blue Jeans.
- ☐ Bohemian/Artistic.
- ☐ Skate/Surf.
- ☐ Flashy.
- ☐ Other ______________.

Circumstances that put me at peace or destress me are:

______________________________ ______________________________

______________________________ ______________________________

Things that give me an adrenaline rush are:

______________________________ ______________________________

______________________________ ______________________________

Things that make me feel safe and secure are:

______________________________ ______________________________

______________________________ ______________________________

Things that are part of my daily routine are:

______________________________ ______________________________

______________________________ ______________________________

Things I enjoy doing during the week are:

______________________________ ______________________________

______________________________ ______________________________

Things I enjoy doing on the weekend are:

______________________________ ______________________________

______________________________ ______________________________

I would describe my dream house and place to live as:

______________________________ ______________________________

______________________________ ______________________________

WHAT I VALUE

Dining, Movies, Music And Media

I am an adventurous eater.	☐ yes	☐ no	☐ sometimes
I like to share my food with others.	☐ yes	☐ no	☐ sometimes
I mind others eating off of my fork.	☐ yes	☐ no	☐ sometimes
I mind others drinking from my glass.	☐ yes	☐ no	☐ sometimes

I enjoy eating or would be willing to try the following types of cuisine: (Check all that apply.)

☐ Chinese.	☐ Mexican.	☐ American.	☐ Indian.
☐ Spanish.	☐ Fusion.	☐ Portuguese.	☐ Japanese.
☐ Sushi.	☐ Caribbean.	☐ Soul.	☐ Fast Food.
☐ Italian.	☐ Southern.	☐ Gourmet.	☐ French.
☐ Seafood.	☐ Egyptian.	☐ African.	☐ ________________________.

Once I tried: (type of food) ______________________________________ **and loved it!**

Once I tried: (type of food) ______________________________________ **and despised it!**

Foods that I am allergic to:

______________________________ ______________________________

______________________________ ______________________________

Foods I enjoy cooking:

______________________________ ______________________________

______________________________ ______________________________

My ideal place(s) for a quiet/romantic dinner would be:

______________________________ ______________________________

______________________________ ______________________________

My ideal place(s) for a casual dinner would be:

______________________________ ______________________________

______________________________ ______________________________

My ideal place(s) for a picnic would be:

______________________________ ______________________________

______________________________ ______________________________

Dining, Movies, Music And Media

The number of times in a year I like to or would like to attend:

a musical is	___ **0-2 times.**	___ **3-5 times.**	___ **6+ times.**
a theatrical performance is	___ **0-2 times.**	___ **3-5 times.**	___ **6+ times.**
an off-broadway show is	___ **0-2 times.**	___ **3-5 times.**	___ **6+ times.**
a movie is	___ **0-2 times.**	___ **3-5 times.**	___ **6+ times.**
a concert is	___ **0-2 times.**	___ **3-5 times.**	___ **6+ times.**

Types of movies I like:

Movies I saw and loved:

Movies I saw and did not like:

Types of performances I like:

Specific performances I saw and loved:

Specific performances I saw and did not like:

Dining, Movies, Music And Media

Types of concerts I like:

______________________ ______________________
______________________ ______________________
______________________ ______________________

Concerts I saw and loved:

______________________ ______________________
______________________ ______________________
______________________ ______________________

Concerts I saw and did not like:

______________________ ______________________
______________________ ______________________
______________________ ______________________

The types of music I enjoy listening to when I am happy are:

- ☐ Country.
- ☐ Classic Rock.
- ☐ Alternative.
- ☐ Rap.
- ☐ Blues.
- ☐ Pop.
- ☐ Metal.
- ☐ Classical.
- ☐ Inspirational.
- ☐ Disco.
- ☐ Oldies.
- ☐ Instrumental.
- ☐ Jazz.
- ☐ Punk.
- ☐ New Age.
- ☐ Adult Contemporary.
- ☐ Other ______________________.

The types of music I enjoy listening to when I am sad or down are:

- ☐ Country.
- ☐ Classic Rock.
- ☐ Alternative.
- ☐ Rap.
- ☐ Blues.
- ☐ Pop.
- ☐ Metal.
- ☐ Classical.
- ☐ Inspirational.
- ☐ Disco.
- ☐ Oldies.
- ☐ Instrumental.
- ☐ Jazz.
- ☐ Punk.
- ☐ New Age.
- ☐ Adult Contemporary.
- ☐ Other ______________________.

The types of music I like to sing in public or private are:

- ☐ Country.
- ☐ Classic Rock.
- ☐ Alternative.
- ☐ Rap.
- ☐ Blues.
- ☐ Pop.
- ☐ Metal.
- ☐ Classical.
- ☐ Inspirational.
- ☐ Disco.
- ☐ Oldies.
- ☐ Instrumental.
- ☐ Jazz.
- ☐ Punk.
- ☐ New Age.
- ☐ Adult Contemporary.
- ☐ Other ______________________.

Dining, Movies, Music And Media

Magazines I like:

Newspapers/newsletters I like:

Types or topics of books I like:

Types or topics of books, magazines or publications I have no desire to read are:

A book I read and loved was: ____________________

A book I read and did not enjoy: ____________________

I am open to reading new things.	☐ yes	☐ no	☐ sometimes
I like to make time during the week to read.	☐ yes	☐ no	☐ sometimes
I like to discuss with my partner what I read.	☐ yes	☐ no	☐ sometimes
I like to discuss with others what I read.	☐ yes	☐ no	☐ sometimes

WHAT I VALUE

Travel, Sports And Activities

Activities I like to do on a Saturday:

Activities I like to do on a Sunday:

I enjoy the following outdoor activities:

Seasonal activities I enjoy doing in the Winter:

Seasonal activities I enjoy doing in the Spring:

Seasonal activities I enjoy doing in the Summer:

Seasonal activities I enjoy doing in the Autumn:

Travel, Sports And Activities

Activities that I haven't tried, but would like to are:

________________________ ________________________
________________________ ________________________
________________________ ________________________

Activities I would not enjoy or would be resistant to trying:

________________________ ________________________
________________________ ________________________
________________________ ________________________

Activities I've done, and would enjoy doing with my partner:

________________________ ________________________
________________________ ________________________
________________________ ________________________

My favorite sport to watch:

________________________ ________________________
________________________ ________________________
________________________ ________________________

My favorite sport to play:

________________________ ________________________
________________________ ________________________
________________________ ________________________

Team sports that I participate or participated in:

________________________ ________________________
________________________ ________________________
________________________ ________________________

When it comes to sports, the amount of time I dedicate in my day and the level of importance to me to: (Use 1 to indicate what is LEAST important to you and 4 to indicate what is MOST important.)

watch sports at home is	____ hours.	___ 1	___ 2	___ 3	___ 4
watch sports out/with friends/at a bar is	____ hours.	___ 1	___ 2	___ 3	___ 4
attend seasonal games is	____ hours.	___ 1	___ 2	___ 3	___ 4

Travel, Sports And Activities

When booking a trip with my partner, I prefer to travel with:

☐ just my partner. ☐ my partner and my friends. ☐ my partner and family.

In a given year, the percentage of time I would want to travel:

with just my partner is ____%. with new people is ____%. with just my friends is ____%. alone is ____%.

When traveling with my partner, the amount of time I like to spend during the trip:

with just my partner is ____%. with new people is ____%. with just my friends is ____%. alone is ____%.

Places I've traveled to and enjoyed are:

______________________ ______________________
______________________ ______________________
______________________ ______________________

Places I've traveled to and did not enjoy:

______________________ ______________________
______________________ ______________________
______________________ ______________________

Places I would like to travel to:

______________________ ______________________
______________________ ______________________
______________________ ______________________

Places I have visited but would love to see again with my partner:

______________________ ______________________
______________________ ______________________
______________________ ______________________

My favorite vacation spots are:

______________________ ______________________
______________________ ______________________
______________________ ______________________

When considering a trip, I primarily make my decision based on:

☐ climate. ☐ activities. ☐ shopping. ☐ cultural experiences.
☐ proximity. ☐ night life. ☐ history. ☐ educational experiences.

Hobbies, Skills And Interests

My talents: (A talent is a natural ability.)

Talents I wish I had:

Skills I have: (A skill is a process you've learned.)

Skills I'd like to learn:

My hobbies:

New hobbies I'd like to take up:

New skills or hobbies I'd like to learn with my partner:

Romance And What It Means To Me

My need for my partner to show me signs of affection is:

☐ daily. ☐ weekly. ☐ monthly. ☐ when he/she remembers.

I like to show my partner simple signs of my affection:

☐ daily. ☐ weekly. ☐ monthly. ☐ when I remember.

My need for my partner to tell me that I am loved and appreciated is:

☐ daily. ☐ weekly. ☐ monthly. ☐ when he/she remembers.

My need to be intimate with my partner to "maintain a connection" to him/her is:

☐ daily. ☐ weekly. ☐ monthly. ☐ unnecessary.

I define romance as:

____

____

____

After a romantic moment, I like to:

____

____

____

After a romantic moment, the best thing my partner could do is:

____

____

____

After a romantic moment, the worst thing my partner could do is:

____

____

____

Romance And What It Means To Me

In order for me to bond romantically with my partner I must feel that:

My idea of a romantic kiss is:

My idea of a romantic hug is:

The quickest way for my partner to get me into a romantic mood is:

A romantic fantasy I have is:

It is important to me that romantically my partner and I make time for:

Romance And What It Means To Me

Things that put me in a romantic mood:

Places or settings that put me in a romantic mood:

Activities that put me in a romantic mood:

Music that puts me in a romantic mood:

Food/beverages that put me in a romantic mood:

Things or actions that will immediately ruin a romantic mood for me are:

Romance And What It Means To Me

My idea of acceptable public affection is:

______________________________ ______________________________
______________________________ ______________________________
______________________________ ______________________________

My level of comfort with public affection is: ___ 1 ___ 2 ___ 3 ___ 4
(Use 1 to indicate UNCOMFORTABLE and 4 to indicate COMFORTABLE to you.)

I am someone who:

- ☐ finds time for romance with my partner, even in the course of a daily routine.
- ☐ has to be in the right frame of mind to be romantic with my partner.
- ☐ has to plan or designate time for romance.

My idea of a romantic evening with my partner is:

____
____
____

My idea of a romantic weekend with my partner is:

____
____
____

Something romantic my partner could do for my birthday or special occasion is:

____
____
____

Something romantic my partner could do for me if I've had a long day or a hard day is:

____
____
____

Romance And What It Means To Me

When it comes to romance, I like it when my partner:

The type of communication I need with my partner to feel romantically connected is:

- ☐ minimal.
- ☐ attentive.
- ☐ affectionate.
- ☐ unimportant.

When out with other couples, friends or co-workers, the type of attention and interaction I'd like my partner to maintain with me or show me so that I feel comfortable in a group is:

- ☐ minimal.
- ☐ attentive.
- ☐ affectionate.
- ☐ unimportant.

The aspects of a relationship that I love:

The aspects of a relationship that I least enjoy:

Romance And What It Means To Me

The best manner in which my partner could respectfully give me romantic guidance would be to

☐ talk to me and say:

☐ show me by:

☐ leave me a note and explain to me that:

When I feel betrayed, I typically:

Situations or actions that could cause me to stray from my relationship with my partner are:

If I experience any of the following, I could never reconnect romantically with my partner:

WHAT I VALUE

Romance And What It Means To Me

If my partner feels romantically disconnected with me because of something I am doing, I would:

☐ be willing to talk and adjust my behavior. ☐ not be willing to talk and/or adjust my behavior.

The way he/she could bring this up is:

____

____

____

Things that will immediately or over time disconnect me romantically from my partner are:

- ☐ flirting with others.
- ☐ smoking.
- ☐ speaking to me in a disrespectful manner.
- ☐ being moody or not communicating with me
- ☐ arguing in public with me.
- ☐ embarrassing me.
- ☐ being demanding of me.
- ☐ referencing previous personal relationships.
- ☐ referencing the physical attributes of others.
- ☐ referencing romantic fantasies with others.
- ☐ spending too much time with co-workers.
- ☐ consistently being stressed or in a bad mood.
- ☐ not maintaining his/her appearance.
- ☐ not appreciating my interests.
- ☐ not appreciating my activities.
- ☐ not wanting me to spend time with my friends.
- ☐ not wanting me to spend time with my family.
- ☐ not having an appreciation for my talents.
- ☐ bringing up past mistakes I've made.
- ☐ not apologizing for hurting my feelings.
- ☐ being insensitive or cold.
- ☐ not wanting me to spend money on myself.
- ☐ raising his/her voice to me.
- ☐ getting drunk.
- ☐ taking recreational drugs.
- ☐ not including me with friends.
- ☐ ignoring me in public.
- ☐ making me nervous.
- ☐ going to functions, events without me.
- ☐ traveling on vacation without me.
- ☐ always talking about work.
- ☐ spending excessive time with his/her friends.
- ☐ not having an appreciation for my time.
- ☐ telling lies, half truths or stories.
- ☐ not maintaining his/her personal hygiene.
- ☐ not supporting my dreams.
- ☐ discouraging me.
- ☐ being unappreciative of me.
- ☐ not wanting me to spend time alone.
- ☐ nagging me/being overbearing.
- ☐ not giving me closure.
- ☐ not wanting me to spend time on sports.
- ☐ rarely planning "us" time.
- ☐ restricting my personal purchases.

Romance And What It Means To Me

Things that keep me romantically engaged and involved with my partner are:

- ☐ flirting with me.
- ☐ preparing or picking up dinner for us.
- ☐ bringing me breakfast in bed.
- ☐ teaching me a sport he/she likes.
- ☐ cooking with me.
- ☐ dancing with me.
- ☐ leaving me love notes.
- ☐ showing me he/she appreciates me.
- ☐ making reservations at a quiet restaurant.
- ☐ kissing me at least once a day.
- ☐ putting his/her arms around me.
- ☐ planning an activity for just the two of us.
- ☐ touching my hair or face.
- ☐ ironing my clothes.
- ☐ telling me I'm loved.
- ☐ watching television together.
- ☐ giving me compliments in public.
- ☐ sending me flowers.
- ☐ being playful with me.
- ☐ teaching me an activity he/she likes.
- ☐ designating a weekly date night.
- ☐ giving me a massage.
- ☐ learning a new skill with me.
- ☐ running me a bath.
- ☐ planning a special night in with me.
- ☐ hugging me at least once a day.
- ☐ holding my hand.
- ☐ planning a picnic with me.
- ☐ going for a walk together.
- ☐ ordering dinner for me.
- ☐ telling me I'm appreciated.
- ☐ telling me I'm cherished.
- ☐ reading together.
- ☐ going out of his/her way to help me.

Actions by my partner that would end our relationship would be:

______________________________ ______________________________
______________________________ ______________________________
______________________________ ______________________________

Actions that I consider to be disrespectful to me when exhibited by my partner that could cause me to shut down romantically are:

______________________________ ______________________________
______________________________ ______________________________
______________________________ ______________________________

Actions exhibited by my partner that I may misinterpret as being disrespectful are:

______________________________ ______________________________
______________________________ ______________________________
______________________________ ______________________________

Communication Tip: Take a look below at how your partner's communication style helps identify what she values, is drawn to and thrives on. Now review her answers in the **What I Value** section. You'll notice how her current communication style often drives the types of activities, events and social interactions she enjoys most.

Go-Getter Traits **This style is:** ☐ my primary style. ☐ my secondary style.
What she values most: accomplishment, achievement, winning and leadership
What she thrives on: seeing results in a short amount of time
What she is drawn to: adventure, new challenges, exploring and variety
How to make plans with her: tell her the key points what, where, when and how

Perfectionist Traits **This style is:** ☐ my primary style. ☐ my secondary style.
What she values most: knowledge, learning, responsibility and truth
What she thrives on: the ability to learn new things, maintain quality and accuracy
What she is drawn to: history, serenity, defined tasks and visual attractions
How to make plans with her: put plans in writing, with specific details and defined tasks

Enthusiast Traits **This style is:** ☐ my primary style. ☐ my secondary style.
What she values most: recognition, prestige, approval, respect and justice
What she thrives on: friendly people, the ability to help others, sharing ideas
What she is drawn to: freedom from details, fun projects and social activities
How to make plans with her: be spontaneous, talk about 2 to 3 options of fun things to do

Nurturer Traits **This style is:** ☐ my primary style. ☐ my secondary style.
What she values most: security, lasting relationships, inner peace and belonging
What she thrives on: having quality relationships, security and time to adjust
What she is drawn to: relaxation, freedom from stress, team work, friends, security
How to make plans with her: ask her in advance how she feels about a given activity

WHERE I STAND

When You Complete This Section You Will Learn:

- ✓ How Your Core Values Impact Your Daily Actions
- ✓ How Your Beliefs Drive Your Conduct

Section Goal: Reveal What Drives You

For a moment, consider all of the sources that have influenced your core values throughout your life, such as family, friends, teachers, colleagues, social groups, religious organizations, schooling and culture. This section is intended to reveal how your beliefs and core values have guided the development of your character. Recognizing the compatibility of your and your partner's core values can be a new opportunity for positive growth in your relationship.

When You Exchange Your Workbook, Your Partner Will Learn:

Relationship Expectations

In the course of a week the amount of time I hoped to spend with my partner would be: _____ hours.

In the course of a week the amount of time I hoped to spend alone would be: _____ hours.

I always hoped that my daily routine with my partner would include:

I always hoped that my holidays with my partner would involve:

I always hoped that my traveling with my partner would involve:

I always hoped that my romantic time with my partner would involve:

WHERE I STAND

Relationship Expectations

In the course of a week the amount of time I hoped to spend with friends would be: _____ hours.

In the course of a week the amount of time I hoped to spend with my family would be: _____ hours.

I always hoped that my activities with my partner would include:

____

____

____

____

____

____

I always hoped that at the end of my work day, I:

____

____

____

____

____

____

I always hoped that my routine when I got home from work would include:

____

____

____

____

____

____

I always hoped that at the end of my work day my partner would:

____

____

____

____

____

____

WHERE I STAND

Religion And Politics

I consider myself to be a spiritual person. ☐ yes ☐ no ☐ sometimes
I consider myself to be a religious person. ☐ yes ☐ no ☐ sometimes

The religion I was raised to practice was: ____________________
The religion I currently practice is: ____________________
The religion I prefer my family to practice is: ____________________

The level of importance to me regarding me attending regular religious services is:
☐ unimportant. ☐ somewhat important. ☐ extremely important.

The level of importance to me regarding my partner attending regular religious services with me is:
☐ unimportant. ☐ somewhat important. ☐ extremely important.

The level of importance to me regarding me celebrating religious holidays is:
☐ unimportant. ☐ somewhat important. ☐ extremely important.

The level of importance to me regarding my partner celebrating religious holidays with me:
☐ unimportant. ☐ somewhat important. ☐ extremely important.

My political affiliation or party is: ____________________

The level of importance of me following politics is:
☐ unimportant. ☐ somewhat important. ☐ extremely important.

The level of importance of me being politically active is:
☐ unimportant. ☐ somewhat important. ☐ extremely important.

The level of importance of me discussing my political views with others is:
☐ unimportant ☐ somewhat important. ☐ extremely important.

The level of importance of me and my partner sharing the same political views is:
☐ unimportant. ☐ somewhat important. ☐ extremely important.

WHERE I STAND

Charity, Volunteering And Community Involvement

I consider giving financially to charitable organizations to be:

☐ unimportant. ☐ somewhat important. ☐ extremely important.

I consider volunteering my time or talents to charitable organizations to be:

☐ unimportant. ☐ somewhat important. ☐ extremely important.

The amount of time in a month that I dedicate to volunteering my time/talents is:

☐ 0-5 hours. ☐ 6-12 hours. ☐ 13+ hours.

The amount of money I believe I should give to charitable causes in a year is:

☐ none. ☐ under $500. ☐ over $500.

Charities/organizations I support financially:

______________________ ______________________
______________________ ______________________
______________________ ______________________

Charities/organizations I support with my time or talents:

______________________ ______________________
______________________ ______________________
______________________ ______________________

Social/special interest/organization memberships I have:

______________________ ______________________
______________________ ______________________
______________________ ______________________

Charities/organizations I would like to support:

______________________ ______________________
______________________ ______________________
______________________ ______________________

WHERE I STAND

Career And Finances

The amount of time I need to commit to my job or career in a given day is:

☐ under 8 hours. ☐ 8 hours. ☐ 8+ hours.

Being happy at my job/career choice is:

☐ unimportant. ☐ somewhat important. ☐ extremely important.

The degree to which my job utilizes my talents and skills is:

☐ unimportant. ☐ somewhat important. ☐ extremely important.

The importance that my job has room for financial growth is:

☐ unimportant. ☐ somewhat important. ☐ extremely important.

The importance that my job has room for skill development is:

☐ unimportant. ☐ somewhat important. ☐ extremely important.

I am happy with my current job/career choice.

☐ yes ☐ no ☐ unimportant

I am satisfied with my salary.

☐ yes ☐ no ☐ unimportant

If I could have any job or career it would be:

____

____

The reason why I am not doing that career now is:

____

____

If I wanted to change my career or make more money, I would have to:

____

____

WHERE I STAND

Career And Finances

Career goals I have and would like to accomplish within one year are:

Career goals I have and would like to accomplish within five years are:

Career goals I have and would like to accomplish within ten years are:

Financial goals I have and would like to accomplish within one year are:

Financial goals I have and would like to accomplish within five years are:

Financial goals I have and would like to accomplish within ten years are:

A dream I have is to one day is to:

WHERE I STAND

Career And Finances

I believe when it comes to finances in a living arrangement with my partner:

☐ I	☐ my partner	☐ both of us	**should control the finances.**
☐ I	☐ my partner	☐ both of us	**should pay the monthly bills.**
☐ I	☐ my partner	☐ both of us	**should earn the income.**
☐ I	☐ my partner	☐ both of us	**should set up a budget.**
☐ I	☐ my partner	☐ both of us	**should save money.**

I'm most comfortable with having joint bank accounts to pay bills.

☐ yes ☐ no ☐ unimportant ☐ would consider it

I'm most comfortable with having a "war chest".

☐ yes ☐ no ☐ unimportant ☐ would consider it

I'm most comfortable with keeping my own finances separate from my partner's.

☐ yes ☐ no ☐ unimportant ☐ would consider it

I'm most comfortable with contributing part of my earnings and keeping part for myself.

☐ yes ☐ no ☐ unimportant ☐ would consider it

I'm most comfortable if we are both working, both incomes should contribute to the bills.

☐ yes ☐ no ☐ unimportant ☐ would consider it

I'm most comfortable if we are both working, both incomes should contribute to luxury purchases.

☐ yes ☐ no ☐ unimportant ☐ would consider it

When I want to splurge on myself, I:

____

____

When I want to splurge on others, I:

____

____

WHERE I STAND

Career And Finances

I believe major purchases should be decided:

☐ by me. ☐ by my partner. ☐ jointly.

I believe that having good credit is:

☐ unimportant. ☐ somewhat important. ☐ extremely important.

I believe that knowing how to properly balance a checkbook is:

☐ unimportant. ☐ somewhat important. ☐ extremely important.

I believe that paying bills on time is:

☐ unimportant. ☐ somewhat important. ☐ extremely important.

I believe that saving money is:

☐ unimportant. ☐ somewhat important. ☐ extremely important.

I believe that investing money is:

☐ unimportant. ☐ somewhat important. ☐ extremely important.

I believe that planning for retirement is:

☐ unimportant. ☐ somewhat important. ☐ extremely important.

I believe that planning a budget for everyday living is:

☐ unimportant. ☐ somewhat important. ☐ extremely important.

Monthly, the amount of money I think is acceptable to spend on:

a car	________	a home	________
luxury items	________	clothing	________
home maintenance	________	personal grooming	________
dining/entertainment	________	hobbies/interests	________
special events	________	gifts	________
travel	________	furnishings	________
insurance	________	investments	________
children	________	education	________

Career And Finances

If my partner made enough money to support the both of us or our family I would still want to work.

☐ yes ☐ no ☐ unimportant ☐ would consider it

My career or business drives my life.

☐ yes ☐ no ☐ sometimes

I make emotionally based purchases.

☐ yes ☐ no ☐ sometimes

When it comes to money, I tend to be:

☐ a spender. ☐ a saver. ☐ budget conscious.

Positive aspects of my career:

______________________________ ______________________________
______________________________ ______________________________
______________________________ ______________________________

Negative aspects of my career:

______________________________ ______________________________
______________________________ ______________________________
______________________________ ______________________________

To change the negatives, I would have to:

______________________________ ______________________________
______________________________ ______________________________
______________________________ ______________________________

If I never had to work again, I would spend my time doing things like:

______________________________ ______________________________
______________________________ ______________________________
______________________________ ______________________________

WHERE I STAND

Managing Time

The importance of spending time daily with my children/family is:

☐ unimportant. ☐ somewhat important. ☐ extremely important.

The importance of spending time weekly with my children/family is:

☐ unimportant. ☐ somewhat important. ☐ extremely important.

The importance of spending time daily with my friends is:

☐ unimportant. ☐ somewhat important. ☐ extremely important.

The importance of spending time weekly with my friends is:

☐ unimportant. ☐ somewhat important. ☐ extremely important.

My relationship with my father/father figure was or is:

☐ like a parent. ☐ like a friend. ☐ distant/estranged.

My relationship with my mother/mother figure was or is:

☐ like a parent. ☐ like a friend. ☐ distant/estranged.

I am closer to my friends than to my family.

☐ yes ☐ no

I consider my friends to be my family.

☐ yes ☐ no

It's perfectly okay to password protect my e-mail and cell phone for privacy from my partner.

☐ yes ☐ no

When I need advice or someone to confide in, I typically go to: ______________________________

My best friend is having a bachelor/bachelorette party in Las Vegas. My attitude is I am:

☐ attending and "*what happens in Vegas stays in Vegas.*"

☐ attending but it's not my style to get caught up in the moment.

☐ not attending because my partner is uncomfortable with the idea.

☐ not attending as I am not interested in what it has to offer.

Managing Time

The level of importance of my spending time daily with my pet(s) is:

☐ unimportant. ☐ somewhat important. ☐ extremely important.

The level of importance of my partner treating my pet(s) the same as I do is:

☐ unimportant. ☐ somewhat important. ☐ extremely important.

The level of importance of my partner liking my pet(s) is:

☐ unimportant. ☐ somewhat important. ☐ extremely important.

Pets I am willing to own or live with:

________________________ ________________________

________________________ ________________________

________________________ ________________________

________________________ ________________________

I treat my pet(s) like they are:

☐ pets. ☐ children. ☐ animals.

I am most comfortable keeping my pet(s):

☐ outside in a fenced yard. ☐ in cages. ☐ in cages sometimes.

☐ outside all of the time. ☐ full reign inside. ☐ in restricted areas inside.

When I travel I am most comfortable with my pet(s):

☐ being boarded. ☐ with a pet sitter. ☐ coming along.

The amount of money I think is acceptable to spend on my pet(s):

grooming __________ healthcare __________

toys/treats __________ living quarters __________

I allow my pet(s) to sleep on my bed/ furniture. ☐ yes ☐ no ☐ would consider it

I allow my pet(s) to be in all areas of my home. ☐ yes ☐ no ☐ would consider it

I allow my pet(s) to roam freely outside. ☐ yes ☐ no ☐ would consider it

I allow my pet(s) to eat table food. ☐ yes ☐ no ☐ would consider it

WHERE I STAND

My Views On General Issues

My view of having children is:

☐ I want children. ☐ I'm not sure. ☐ I don't want children.

I believe having children should be planned.

☐ yes ☐ no ☐ either

I am in favor of the philosophy "spare the rod, spoil the child."

☐ yes ☐ no

My foremost concern for my child/children is or would be the development of:

☐ education. ☐ business skills. ☐ sports/talents. ☐ trade skills.

If my child was born with a physical handicap, the way I would handle it is:

____

____

____

I believe when people get divorced and children are involved, parents should:

____

____

____

I believe children should be disciplined in the following way:

____

____

____

If I learned that my partner had an affair I would:

____

____

____

WHERE I STAND

My Views On General Issues

In the course of the day I spend: _______ hours with my child/children. (if applicable)

In the course of the day I believe myself and my partner should spend: _______ hours with my/his/her children. (if applicable)

I believe that I, as the parent or parents in general should decide their child's/children's education.

☐ yes ☐ no

I believe that I, as the parent or parents in general should decide their child's/children's religion.

☐ yes ☐ no

I believe that I, as the parent or parents in general should decide their child's/children's friends.

☐ yes ☐ no

I believe that I, as the parent or parents in general should randomly check through their child's/ children's room and personal belongings.

☐ yes ☐ no

I believe that I, as the parent or parents in general should openly discuss the following subjects with their children:

☐ drugs.	☐ alcohol.	☐ promiscuous behavior.	☐ dating.
☐ sexual abuse.	☐ physical abuse.	☐ other religions.	☐ violence.
☐ bullying.	☐ death.	☐ other cultures.	☐ illness/disease.
☐ sexual preference.	☐ genders.	☐ physical challenges.	☐ etiquette/manners.
☐ pregnancy.	☐ my past.	☐ controversial topics.	☐ other _____________.

I believe in exposing my child/children to: (if applicable)

☐ education.	☐ business skills.	☐ sports/talents.	☐ trade skills.
☐ art.	☐ music.	☐ science.	☐ history.
☐ nature.	☐ astronomy.	☐ computers.	☐ language.
☐ philosophy.	☐ current affairs.	☐ legal issues.	☐ medicine/technology.
☐ cooking.	☐ other cultures.	☐ politics.	☐ other _____________.

My Views On General Issues

I believe you can have one love or one partner for life.

☐ yes ☐ no

I believe marriage should be a renewable commitment on a five or ten year basis.

☐ yes ☐ no

In order for me to be intimate with someone, I have to be emotionally connected to him/her.

☐ yes ☐ no

In order for me to be intimate with someone, I have to be mentally connected to him/her.

☐ yes ☐ no

I believe it is acceptable to want other singles or couples to participate in my romantic life.

☐ yes ☐ no

I am a firm believer of telling people what they want to hear to keep them happy and to avoid confrontation - even if it means bending the truth a bit.

☐ yes ☐ no

If I could rob a bank and never get caught, I would do it.

☐ yes ☐ no ☐ would consider it

I believe it's natural for people in a relationship to be monogamous.

☐ yes ☐ no ☐ would consider it

I think it is okay to break the law sometimes.

☐ yes ☐ no ☐ would consider it

I often make right turns on red even when there's a sign that says not to.

☐ yes ☐ no ☐ would consider it

I would consider dating or marrying someone with children from a previous marriage.

☐ yes ☐ no ☐ would consider it

WHERE I STAND

My Views On General Issues

If I bought a pet with a partner and we split up, I think the pet should go with:

If I hit a $10 million lottery, things I would do with the money would be:

If I was in charge of giving $10 million to charities or non-profit organizations, I would give to:

I would expect my partner to forgive me for having any type of romantic involvement outside of our relationship if it was with: (for example the name of a rock star, model, movie star, old lover, etc.)

If I learned that my partner and I were pregnant and I was not prepared to have a child I would:

If I found out that my partner was keeping secrets from me I would:

If my partner had a fling after drinking too much I would:

Communication Tip: The answers in this section will help you better understand where your partner stands on key issues. Remember her past experiences and core values have shaped her current beliefs. By reading the information below you'll learn how your partner builds and perceives trust with you and others based on the traits of her communication style.

Go-Getter Traits **This style is:** ☐ my primary style. ☐ my secondary style.

Her time focus: immediate, now
Her questioning style: debating - what
Draws conclusions: quickly, impulsively
Avoid: looking bored
Content of speech: events
Basis for trust: experiences

Perfectionist Traits **This style is:** ☐ my primary style. ☐ my secondary style.

Her time focus: past, historical
Her questioning style: questions - how
Draws conclusions: slow, cautious
Avoid: being inaccurate
Content of speech: things
Basis for trust: credibility

Enthusiast Traits **This style is:** ☐ my primary style. ☐ my secondary style.

Her time focus: future, visionary
Her questioning style: probing - possibilities
Draws conclusions: spontaneous, intuitive
Avoid: repetition/rejection
Content of speech: improvements
Basis for trust: commitments

Nurturer Traits **This style is:** ☐ my primary style. ☐ my secondary style.

Her time focus: present, current
Her questioning style: inquiring - your opinion
Draws conclusions: moderate, cooperative
Avoid: conflict
Content of speech: people
Basis for trust: rapport

WHERE

WHEN I FEEL APPRECIATED

When You Complete This Section <u>You</u> Will Learn:

- ✓ **Ways You Want Your Partner To Relate To You**
- ✓ **How Your Beliefs Drive Your Conduct**

<u>Section Goal:</u> Define How You Want To Be Treated

In this section you'll define how your partner can best express his/her appreciation, affection and support for you from <u>YOUR</u> frame of reference. When you and your partner each know how to effectively communicate an understanding of the other's values, it will strengthen your relationship. You and your partner can refer to this section in each others' guides when you want to learn the most accurate way to demonstrate your respect and appreciation for each other.

When You Exchange Your Workbook, <u>Your Partner</u> Will Learn:

WHEN I FEEL APPRECIATED

Quick "Pick Me Ups"

When I'm feeling defeated, the thing I need to hear most from my partner is:

When I'm feeling sad, something my partner could do is:

When I'm feeling angry, the best way my partner could react is:

When I'm feeling overwhelmed with work, something my partner could do is:

When I achieve a special goal, my partner could help me celebrate my success by:

Something my partner could do to make me smile is:

Something thoughtful my partner could do on my birthday would be:

Something thoughtful my partner could do on our anniversary would be:

Something thoughtful my partner could do in general would be:

WHEN I FEEL APPRECIATED

My Favorites

When my partner remembers my favorite things it puts me in a good mood and shows me that he/she truly appreciates me. They are:

color ______________________

perfume/cologne ______________________

scent ______________________

lucky number ______________________

flower/plant ______________________

type of pet is or was ______________________

place to clear my head ______________________

thing to do on a Saturday ______________________

thing to do on a Sunday ______________________

subject to read about ______________________

type of movie ______________________

topic to search the internet ______________________

type of job is or was ______________________

place of interest ______________________

vacation spot ______________________

activity I like to do ______________________

sport I like to do ______________________

sports type and team ______________________

restaurant and/or bar ______________________

fast food ______________________

comfort food ______________________

dessert ______________________

alcoholic beverage ______________________

non-alcoholic beverage ______________________

type of television show ______________________

band/musical performance ______________________

WHEN I FEEL APPRECIATED

Simple Signs Of Affection

Quick ways my partner can show me love or appreciation:

Simple things I'd love to do with my partner are:

Places I'd love to go to with my partner are:

If my partner wants to splurge on me he/she could:

WHEN I FEEL APPRECIATED

Simple Signs Of Affection

Ways I like to celebrate my birthday, an achievement or special occasion with my partner:

Ways I like to celebrate holidays with my partner are:

The feelings I love in a relationship:

Issues I need to work on immediately to enjoy a relationship more are:

It's As Easy As 1, 2, 3

Three things that make me smile are:

1. ____
2. ____
3. ____

Three misconceptions I believe people have about me are:

1. ____
2. ____
3. ____

Three things I would like to improve about myself are:

1. ____
2. ____
3. ____

Three ways I interpret respect from others toward me are:

1. ____
2. ____
3. ____

Three things I need to motivate myself are:

1. ____
2. ____
3. ____

It's As Easy As 1, 2, 3

Three ways I interpret loyalty by others, to me are:

1. ______________________________
2. ______________________________
3. ______________________________

Three ways my partner can show me empathy are:

1. ______________________________
2. ______________________________
3. ______________________________

Three ways my partner can show me support are:

1. ______________________________
2. ______________________________
3. ______________________________

Three bad habits I am currently trying to break are:

1. ______________________________
2. ______________________________
3. ______________________________

Three goals I am trying to achieve are:

1. ______________________________
2. ______________________________
3. ______________________________

It's As Easy As 1, 2, 3

Three pet peeves of mine are:

1. ____________________
2. ____________________
3. ____________________

Three things I must do daily to feel good are:

1. ____________________
2. ____________________
3. ____________________

Three things that make me feel uncomfortable are:

1. ____________________
2. ____________________
3. ____________________

Three things I'd enjoy doing with my partner virtually any time are:

1. ____________________
2. ____________________
3. ____________________

WHEN I FEEL APPRECIATED

Dates To Remember

My birth date is: ______________________

Anniversaries:

Family member birthdays:

Special holidays:

Sporting events/important activities:

Other important dates:

Disagreement "Do's" And Please "Do Nots"

I would ask my partner that if

we ever disagree in public, please **DO:**

we ever disagree in public, please **DON'T:**

we disagree on my attire for a specific event or place and you want to tell me, please **DO:**

we ever have a heated discussion or argument, please **DON'T:**

I'm struggling to break a bad habit and we disagree with my method, please **DO:**

you'd like to tell me in advance of your expectations of something or someplace we're going, please **DO:**

I've done something that has offended you or hurt your feelings and you'd like to tell me, please **DO:**

I'm in a bad mood from a disagreement we've had, please **DO:**

Disagreement "Do's" And Please "Do Nots"

I would ask my partner that if

I do something that embarrasses you or makes you feel uncomfortable and you want to tell me, please **DO:**

I do something that embarrasses or makes you feel uncomfortable and you want to tell me, please **DON'T:**

I'm trying to give you a hint in public and you don't understand me, please **DON'T:**

In Need Of Advice

If my partner ever needs to speak to someone I trust for advice regarding relationship, he/she could call:

Name ______ Phone ______

Name ______ Phone ______

Name ______ Phone ______

If my partner ever needs to speak to someone I trust for advice regarding special gift, plan or event for me, he/she could call:

Name ______ Phone ______

Name ______ Phone ______

Name ______ Phone ______

In Case Of Emergency

Medical conditions and allergies I have or have had:

Medications I'm taking:

I or a member of my family has a history of:

Emergency Contacts

People to contact in an emergency situation.

Name ____________________ Phone ____________________

Relationship to me ____________________

Name ____________________ Phone ____________________

Relationship to me ____________________

Name ____________________ Phone ____________________

Relationship to me ____________________

WHEN I FEEL APPRECIATED

Communication Tip: When you genuinely make an effort to communicate with your partner in the style that is most natural to her it creates feelings of being understood, valued, acknowledged and appreciated. Use the information below as a reminder of which approach to communication works best for getting "in-sync" with her primary and secondary styles.

Go-Getter Traits

This style is: ☐ my primary style. ☐ my secondary style.

Acknowledge: her accomplishments
Recognize: her desire to achieve things
Create an opportunity for: her to experience adventure
Offer your help by: asking what tasks can be done
Allow her to: lead topics of discussion, choose activities, take charge
She likes an atmosphere: that lends to high functionality and productivity

Perfectionist Traits

This style is: ☐ my primary style. ☐ my secondary style.

Acknowledge: her knowledge, what she believes
Recognize: her desire to learn
Create an opportunity for: her to see information, facts and details
Offer your help by: asking how can you help and then write it down
Allow her to: provide the order in which things must be done
She likes an atmosphere: that is serene, orderly and neat

Enthusiast Traits

This style is: ☐ my primary style. ☐ my secondary style.

Acknowledge: your respect and approval for what she knows
Recognize: her desire to be fair and make improvements
Create an opportunity for: her to evaluate the pros and cons
Offer your help by: asking what she can show you, so you can help
Allow her to: take a stand on issues
She likes an atmosphere: that is free from details, social and fun

Nurturer Traits

This style is: ☐ my primary style. ☐ my secondary style.

Acknowledge: her need for security
Recognize: her desire for inner peace
Create an opportunity for: her to relax and take her time with things
Offer your help by: asking how can we get this done together
Allow her to: belong to groups and organizations
She likes an atmosphere: that is comfortable and casual

WHY THINGS HAVE AN IMPACT ME

When You Complete This Section You Will Learn:

- ✓ **How Your Past Experiences Have Shaped Your Thinking**
- ✓ **How Your Daily Stressors Effect Your Current Relationship**

 **Section Goal: Become Consciously Aware**

Take a moment and reflect on your life. It has been shaped by years of positive and negative experiences. This section is intended to provide you with an opportunity to discover how your past experiences have an effect the way you relate to and communicate with your partner and others. This is an important section for you and your partner to carefully read. You will each gain a new level of awareness as to how past experiences in your individual lives have an impact on your daily lives as a couple. Thoughtful discussion of these experiences can lead to recognizing how certain learned behaviors may need to be worked on and improved. This section is great for identifying how, when and why you each sometimes need added support and reassurance.

When You Exchange Your Workbook, Your Partner Will Learn:

What I've Learned From Past Relationships

My relationship with my mother figure - positive aspects:

My relationship with my mother figure - negative aspects:

What I need my partner to be most understanding about this relationship is:

WHY THINGS HAVE AN IMPACT ME

What I've Learned From Past Relationships

My relationship with my father figure - positive aspects:

My relationship with my father figure - negative aspects:

What I need my partner to be most understanding about this relationship is:

What I've Learned From Past Relationships

My relationship with my siblings (if applicable) **- positive aspects:**

My relationship with my siblings (if applicable) **- negative aspects:**

What I need my partner to be most understanding about this relationship is:

What I've Learned From Past Relationships

My relationship with my extended family - positive aspects:

My relationship with my extended family - negative aspects:

What I need my partner to be most understanding about this relationship is:

What I've Learned From Past Relationships

My relationship with my childhood friends and schoolmates - positive aspects:

My relationship with my childhood friends and schoolmates - negative aspects:

What I need my partner to be most understanding about this relationship is:

What I've Learned From Past Relationships

My relationship with my children (if applicable) **- positive aspects:**

My relationship with my children (if applicable) **- negative aspects:**

What I need my partner to be most understanding about this relationship is:

What I've Learned From Past Relationships

My last romantic relationship prior to my partner - positive aspects:

My last romantic relationship prior to my partner - negative aspects:

What I need my partner to be most understanding about this relationship is:

Life Lessons I Live By

An experience that has reshaped my behavior and thinking - positive aspects:

An experience that has reshaped my behavior and thinking - negative aspects:

What I need my partner to be most understanding about this experiences is:

Stressors, Fears And Concerns

My three biggest stressors are:

1. ______________________________
2. ______________________________
3. ______________________________

To overcome these stressors, I would have to:

____
____
____

My three biggest personal fears are:

1. ______________________________
2. ______________________________
3. ______________________________

To overcome these personal fears, I would have to:

____
____
____

My three biggest concerns are:

1. ______________________________
2. ______________________________
3. ______________________________

To overcome these concerns, I would have to:

____
____
____

Griefs, Regrets And Disappointments

Past personal griefs that may be impacting my current outlook and/or actions are:

Past personal regrets that may be impacting my current outlook and/or actions are:

Past personal disappointments that may be impacting my current outlook and/or actions are:

Other Situations That Have Had A General Impact On Me

Other situations throughout my life that have had a positive or negative impact on me and may be driving my current actions or reactions:

Other situations throughout my life that have had a positive or negative impact on me and may be driving my current actions or reactions:

Communication Tip: The way in which your partner reacts to situations is a combination of her communication style, past experiences and core values. Understanding the traits below gives you the necessary insight as to how her communication style plays a key role in the way she expresses herself and handles situations.

Go-Getter Traits **This style is:** ☐ my primary style. ☐ my secondary style.

Underlying need: credit, recognition and prestige from achievements
How she handles pressure: takes command to find an end result
How she takes action: controlling, autocratic
How she defends her beliefs: argumentative, persistent, outspoken

Perfectionist Traits **This style is:** ☐ my primary style. ☐ my secondary style.

Underlying need: admiration of accuracy, quality, to be "right" from what she has learned
How she handles pressure: ignores deadlines and pressure situations for the sake of accuracy
How she takes action: slow, methodical
How she defends her beliefs: becomes quiet, disciplined, serious

Enthusiast Traits **This style is:** ☐ my primary style. ☐ my secondary style.

Underlying need: respect, trust and appreciation for her ability to be fair and make improvements
How she handles pressure: attacks when she feels she will look incompetent
How she takes action: spontaneous, quick without paying attention to details
How she defends her beliefs: persuasive, optimistic, motivating

Nurturer Traits **This style is:** ☐ my primary style. ☐ my secondary style.

Underlying need: belonging, security and lasting relationships based on her loyalty
How she handles pressure: too tolerant, caves and gives in to others opinions
How she takes action: asks her peers for opinions first, takes her time
How she defends her beliefs: compromising, considerate, supportive

WHY

HOW I RELATE TO PEOPLE

When You Complete This Section You Will Learn:

- ✓ **What Your Body Language Is Communicating**
- ✓ **If Your Words Are Saying What You Really Mean**

Section Goal: Fine Tune Your Communication

Experience an entirely new level of self-awareness! This section is intended to reveal the true meaning behind your words and body language. It will also address what you and your partner each consider to be acceptable and unacceptable behavior in a relationship. When you and your partner fine tune your ability to recognize the specific cues and clues of your partner's natural communication style, body language and words, it will help each of you to more accurately interpret the other's actions and intentions. Having this clearer understanding can build trust.

When You Exchange Your Workbook, Your Partner Will Learn:

How I Relate To Others In Social Situations

In a social setting, I am at ease when I know:

☐ some people. ☐ a lot of people. ☐ it doesn't matter.

It changes after I've had a few drinks. ☐ yes ☐ no

It changes depending on the crowd. ☐ yes ☐ no

I enjoy hugging people on a social level. ☐ yes ☐ no

I enjoying receiving hugs on a social level. ☐ yes ☐ no

I tend to kiss people hello/goodbye as a friendly gesture after I get to know them.

☐ rarely ☐ periodically ☐ often ☐ all of the time

The types of social gatherings I prefer are:

☐ small groups. ☐ large parties.

When my partner invites me to a social event with his/her friends or co-workers where I know very few people or no one at all, I would feel most comfortable if he/she:

☐ introduces me around.
☐ leaves me to make my own way.
☐ stays by my side.
☐ splits time between myself & attendees.

In most large social situations I am typically:

☐ outgoing.
☐ somewhat social.
☐ in the background.
☐ the life of the party.

In order to feel more at ease in social situations I typically:

☐ have a few drinks.
☐ smoke to relax.
☐ use prescription or recreational drugs.
☐ not applicable.

When I've had too much to drink, I'm typically a:

☐ happy drunk.
☐ sad drunk.
☐ nasty/angry drunk.
☐ sleepy drunk.

How I Relate To Others In Social Situations

I know my partner loves me when he/she says things like:

I know my partner loves me when he/she does things like:

If there is a bad habit I'd like my partner to break, I typically would approach the subject by saying:

If there is something that my partner does that makes me feel uncomfortable, I would bring it up by saying:

If there is something that my partner does that makes me feel great, in order to reinforce that behavior I would probably say:

If there is something that I'd like my partner to do more often, I would bring it up by saying:

How I Relate To Others In Social Situations

If my partner is wearing clothes that may be inappropriate for where we are going or are unbecoming on him/her, typically I would say:

The amount of time I am comfortable conversing with my partner:

- ☐ periodically.
- ☐ often.
- ☐ all the time.

It is easiest to express my feelings:

- ☐ verbally.
- ☐ in writing.
- ☐ in my actions/deeds.

I tend to be humble about:

I tend to be confident about:

When I am embarrassed I tend to:

When I am offended by something or a situation I tend to:

How I Relate To Others In Social Situations

The way my partner can tell that I am feeling happy is:

The way my partner can tell that I am feeling sad is:

The way my partner can tell that I am feeling frustrated is:

The way my partner can tell that I am feeling angry is:

The way my partner can tell that I am feeling inadequate is:

The way my partner can tell that I am feeling insecure is:

The way my partner can tell that I am feeling afraid is:

HOW I RELATE TO PEOPLE

How I Relate To Others In Social Situations

When I am put on the spot, I tend to:

When I get caught in a fib, I tend to:

When I feel pushed into a corner, I usually react by:

When I am wrongly accused, I:

When I am under pressure or have a deadline, I:

When my partner criticizes me, I:

If my partner speaks to or maintains a relationship with his/her "ex," I:

How I Relate To Others In Social Situations

When I am feeling down or defeated I respond best to:

- ☐ a cheering section.
- ☐ being left alone.
- ☐ doing something fun.
- ☐ having my partner say everything will work out.
- ☐ talking about the problem in order to find a solution.
- ☐ other ______________________________.

Things people can say that will build me up are:

______________________ ______________________
______________________ ______________________
______________________ ______________________

Things people say that knock me down:

______________________ ______________________
______________________ ______________________
______________________ ______________________

Things people say that anger me:

______________________ ______________________
______________________ ______________________
______________________ ______________________

Things people do that make me feel uncomfortable:

______________________ ______________________
______________________ ______________________
______________________ ______________________

Emotions I have difficulty expressing:

______________________ ______________________
______________________ ______________________
______________________ ______________________

Communication What I'm Really Saying

Sometimes I'm uncomfortable saying what's on my mind because I am concerned about the way my partner will react, so

when I say: ____

____

what I really mean is: ____

____

when I say: ____

____

what I really mean is: ____

____

when I say: ____

____

what I really mean is: ____

____

when I say: ____

____

what I really mean is: ____

____

Communication What I'm Really Saying

Often my body language and actions will display what I'm feeling inside - even when my words may not. Clues about my body language that will indicate to my partner that I am feeling:

betrayed ____

hurt ____

insecure ____

nervous/afraid ____

frustrated ____

annoyed ____

uncomfortable ____

Defining Time

The percentage of my week I would enjoy spending with:

my partner is ___%. my friends is ___%. my family is ___%. myself/alone is ___%.

The percentage of my week I would enjoy doing an activity with:

my partner is ___%. my friends is ___%. my family is ___%. myself/alone is ___%.

The percentage of my week I would enjoy exercising with:

my partner is ___%. my friends is ___%. my family is ___%. myself/alone is ___%.

I tend to lose my temper.

☐ rarely ☐ periodically ☐ often ☐ all the time

Fighting Fairly

The number of times I have been involved in a physical fight:

as a child is _____. as a teenager is _____. as an adult is _____.

I openly share my thoughts.	☐ yes	☐ no
I am someone who calls names in an argument.	☐ yes	☐ no
I am someone who curses/swears in an argument.	☐ yes	☐ no
I often go with my gut feeling.	☐ yes	☐ no
I often "take digs" or "push buttons" in an argument.	☐ yes	☐ no
I have experienced physical abuse as an adult or child.	☐ yes	☐ no

When I lose my temper I tend to: (Check all that apply.)

☐ get quiet. ☐ get loud. ☐ leave the situation.

☐ confront people. ☐ become aggressive. ☐ become argumentative.

I lose my temper when I feel:

____

____

____

In a disagreement, it drives me crazy when my partner says:

____

____

____

In a disagreement, it drives me crazy when my partner does things such as:

____

____

____

Things that frustrate me are:

____

____

____

Fighting Fairly

I believe that my gut feeling is often: ☐ right. ☐ wrong.

If I know I'm right and the other person is wrong in an argument, I typically:

☐ try to prove my point. ☐ drop it. ☐ discuss both sides.
☐ walk away. ☐ continue arguing. ☐ ______________________.

My typical reaction if someone breaks something of value to me:

____
____
____

My typical reaction if someone takes advantage of me:

____
____
____

My typical reaction if someone hurts my feelings:

____
____
____

My typical reaction if someone disappoints me:

____
____
____

My typical reaction if someone very close to me dies:

____
____
____

Fighting Fairly

Additional information my partner should know about my style of confrontation or way of resolving arguments:

Communication Tip: Your partner's communication style plays a key role in her demeanor, how she speaks, the verbs she uses in conversations and her comfort level when relating to others. You can communicate with your partner more effectively when you get "in sync" with her. To do this adjust your words, tone and pace to match her primary communication style.

Go-Getter Traits

This style is: ☐ my primary style. ☐ my secondary style.

Facial expression: anticipation
Speech: medium pitch, fast, to the point
Body posture: leans forward, aggressive
Wants to know: Can you get it done?
Spacial relation: stand/sit anywhere you can be heard

Connect by using words such as:

- listen
- tell
- announce
- hear me out
- say
- discuss
- mention
- talk to me

Perfectionist Traits

This style is: ☐ my primary style. ☐ my secondary style.

Facial expression: serious
Speech: high pitch, deliberate
Body posture: sits straight up
Wants to know: What do you know?
Spacial relation: sit/stand directly in front of her

Connect by using words such as:

- see
- look
- appear
- clear
- analyze
- discern
- examine
- read

Enthusiast Traits

This style is: ☐ my primary style. ☐ my secondary style.

Facial expression: quick to smile
Speech: low pitch, energetic
Body posture: comfortable, alert
Wants to know: How can you help?
Spacial relation: stand/sit near her side

Connect by using words such as:

- believe
- sense
- imagine
- "I" am
- understand
- pull springs
- hands-on
- take on

Nurturer Traits

This style is: ☐ my primary style. ☐ my secondary style.

Facial expression: calm
Speech: low pitch, calming
Body posture: sits back, relaxed
Wants to know: Who are you?
Spacial relation: stand/sit close to her side

Connect by using words such as:

- comfort
- get in touch with
- smooth
- "we" are
- support
- concrete
- embrace
- hustle

The Most Effective And Useful Guide

To Achieving And Enjoying A Successful Relationship With You!

Congratulations!

If you've taken the time to read and answer all of these questions, congratulations! As you continually review the answers in your and your partner's guide, it will help you:

- ✓ **take proactive efforts towards creating a life that fulfills your needs.**
- ✓ **learn new ways to more effectively communicate with your partner to improve your relationship.**
- ✓ **strengthen your relationship because you'll have a clearer understanding of your own needs and values - as well as those of your partner.**
- ✓ **understand why specific behaviors and actions exist in your relationship.**
- ✓ **clearly identify that your differences in your and your partner's core values, may be indirectly preventing your relationship from flourishing.**

It is now up to you and your partner to make a conscious and daily effort to use your guides as on-going reference tool for improving your communication with, and appreciation for, each other at this stage of your relationship.

The more you and your partner familiarize yourselves with the information in both of your guides, the easier it will be to simplify your relationship by using more effective communication.

ABOUT THE AUTHORS

Candice A. Huddy and T. P. Kenny have drawn on over 30 years of career driven interpersonal communications to co-author the fourth edition revised of "The Complete Reference Guide To Me: The Workbook For Him" and "The Complete Reference Guide To Me: The Workbook For Her."

Candice has a successful 16-year track record as a Creative Director and Strategic Marketing Consultant for Fortune 500 companies, small businesses and professionals.

As a successful business owner, she has used her expertise in consumer relationship-building to help companies reach new customers, increase sales, and drive business by asking the right questions and carefully listening to the needs of business owners and customers. Candice holds a Bachelor of Arts Degree in Communications from Monmouth University.

T. P. Kenny has spent over 15 years in diverse positions in education, law enforcement and the medical field. His advancement throughout his career is a direct result of his expertise in interpersonal communications, methods of instruction and impartial mediation.

As an active member of the International Association of Approved Basketball Officials and the College Basketball Official Association, T. P. has developed his leadership role and mentoring skills through active listening, objective problem solving and team building. T. P. holds a Bachelor of Arts Degree from Lafayette College and a Masters in Physical Therapy from the University of Medicine and Dentistry of New Jersey.

Candice Huddy and T. P. Kenny are involved in many community and charitable activities, including the creation of The WinGate Farms Foundation, Inc., which is an organization dedicated to developing a first-of-its-kind care facility in New Jersey, offering physical, equine and creative therapy programs. This facility will serve children and adults with disabilities to build confidence, knowledge, and agility all in one centralized location. For additional information on "The Complete Reference Guide To Me" or The WinGate Farms Foundation, Inc. visit: **www.TheCompleteReferenceGuideToMe.com** and **www.WinGateFarms.org.**

Professional Communication Strategist

We would like to thank a long-time friend and communication expert, Bill Butcher. Bill has provided professional communication strategies, advice and teaching tools that over the years have had a positive influence on our lives and have lent to the content and development of this workbook.

Bill Butcher, President of Butcher Consulting Group, has over 35 years of experience providing comprehensive executive coaching, interactive training and project consulting for the pharmaceutical, chemical, technical, and professional industries. He has extensive expertise in creating and delivering effective communication, trust-centered leadership, and professional effectiveness seminars. With over 50 copyrights, Bill's unique processes and practical applications have significantly grown four different companies (taking one to over 20 million dollars). Bill has personally coached over 1,250 top tier executives for personal improvement and career advancement, and he has trained over 18,000 professionals in achieving new levels of efficiency and productivity.

Bill received his Bachelors Degree in Chemistry from Dickinson College, Carlisle, PA; course work at Hahnemann Medical School, University of Pennsylvania; and Drexel Graduate Schools in Philadelphia PA. He is a speaker and advisor for numerous organizations, including The New Jersey Council of Teaching Hospitals, Sales and Marketing Executive Institute, the New Jersey Presidents Forum, and the Superior Court System for the State of New Jersey. Bill is involved in many community and charitable activities, including the Salvation Army, Boys and Girls Club and the Children's Psychiatric Clinic. For additional information on Bill Butcher and Butcher Consulting Group, please visit: **www.ButcherConsult.com.**

Biography supplied by Butcher Consulting Group.

Made in the USA
Columbia, SC
05 June 2021

39157517R00080